RIDDLE WORLD

101

Carefully Crafted Riddles, Puns, And Homonyms

David E Hustoft

ISBN 978-1098394189

Design by David E. Hustoft

Cover by David E. Hustoft

First Edition

Available at:
store.bookbaby.com

For
Olivia & Luke

What do you call it when you cover two men with contact cement and push them together?

Male bonding

Why did the man
with low self-esteem
take a rod and reel
to the ketchup and
mustard section of
the supermarket?

He was fishing for
condiments.

For what was the stockbroker arrested while he was working in a large vat of apple juice?

In cider trading.

How did Julius Caesar address the gathering of farmers in Italy's capital when he wanted to borrow their corn?

"Friends, Romans, countrymen, lend me your ears."

What happens when
a bricklayer gets
very frustrated and
gives up on his task?

He throws in the
trowel.

What do you call the feeling of extreme happiness which occurs after reaching the center of an apple?

Core elation.

There was a burglary next door, and I went over to check things out. The police were there and also a serious-looking man who was questioning people and taking notes on a pad. His shirt and pants had pictures of winged flying machines on them. Who was he?

A plane-clothes
detective.

Who does an unborn child call at 2:00 a.m. for a cheeseburger?

Womb service.

What do you call
a large ship that
regularly carries
teeth from one port
to another?

The Tooth Ferry.

What do you call a melody sung while expectorating?

A spit-tune.

What do you call
a very small
Martian?

A Mar-teeny.

What do you call
the long culvert
where female sheep
congregate?

Ewe tube.

What do you call
a creek that is very
self-aware?

Stream of
Consciousness.

What did they call the son of the king after he dyed his face the color of the sky?

Blue Prince.

What do you call a religious graduation ceremony for expert calf-ropers?

A Baca-lariat Service.

What do you call the practice of eating large round shot fired by antique artillery pieces?

Cannonball-ism.

What do you call the imaginary line running north to south through the Rocky Mountains where your bowels involuntarily release?

The Incontinental Divide.

Why did the little boy lift the rabbit-like animal over his head when he heard the scary story?

It was a
hare-raising tale.

What do you call the condition of being born with eyes in your buttocks?

Hind sight.

What do you call a choice made while your body is covered with itchy red welts?

A rash decision.

What do you call
legumes that say
nice things
about you?

Complimentary
peanuts.

What do you call two or more notes played at the same time that cause a parachute to open?

A rip chord.

What do you call
a large plant that
stands guard in front
of a gate and is paid
only one penny?

A cent tree.

What do you call
a reflective surface
for viewing people's
butts?

A rear view mirror.

What do you call
a group of islands
where everybody
eats a Hungarian
stew made of meat
and vegetables,
and flavored with
paprika?

A Goulash Archipelago.

What do you
call quadruplets
motoring around
in a watercraft
while sensing that
something bad is
about to happen?

A feeling of four boating.

What do you call
a street named for
authors who no
longer practice
their craft?

Writer's Block.

What do you call it when a male sheep is very boisterous while bouncing on a mattress on a two-tiered bed?

Ram-bunk-tious.

When you are engaged in archery, what kind of projectiles do you shoot if you are feeling gravely serious?

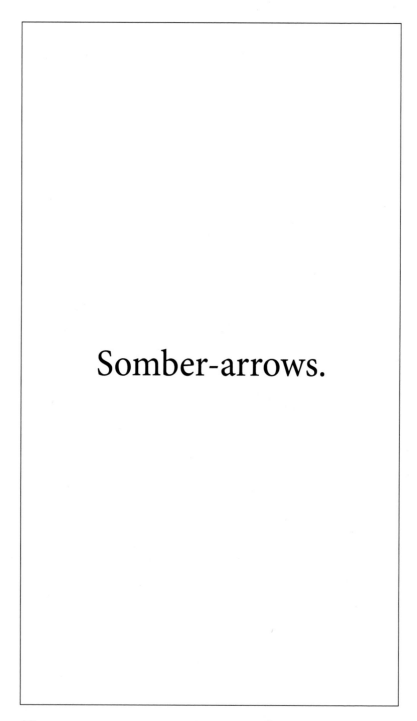

Somber-arrows.

What do you call a person who prepares old yellow cabs so they can be displayed on a wall?

A taxi-dermist.

What do you call a celebrative get-together for small wooden cubes who all live on the same street?

A block party.

What do you call
a person who
smashes and breaks
wooden cubes with
a hammer?

A blockbuster.

What do you call
being in a trance-
like state and seeing
an image of yourself
driving through
a long hole in a
mountain?

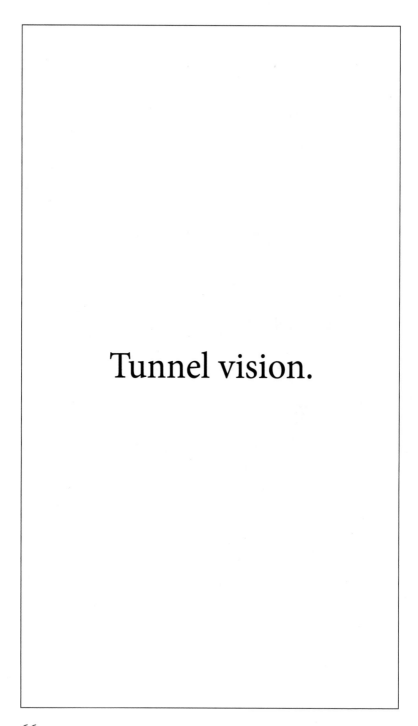

Tunnel vision.

What is the name of the element created when you combine the third of the wise men's gifts with the last name of the only woman to win a Nobel Prize twice?

Myrrh-Curie.

What do you get
when you cross a
tootsie roll with
a mean, mythical
creature that lives
under a bridge and
likes to kick people
in his stocking feet?

A footsie troll.

What do you call it
when a person who
can keep several
balls in the air
at the same time
has an excessively
high opinion of his
appearance, abilities,
and worth?

The juggler vain.

What do you call
it when again
and again you are
without any tiny
pieces of white fuzz
on your clothing
because of your
perseverance?

Re-lint-less.

What do you call
the matriarchal
ruler of a country
that produces only
polyethylene tarps.

The Vis-Queen.

What do you call
a terrifying female
horse ridden by an
armor-clad medieval
soldier?

A knight mare.

What do you call people who focus their hopes and dreams on a deep, water-filled hole in the ground?

Well wishers.

What did the mom and dad melon say to their daughter when she wanted to run off to Las Vegas and get married?

"You can't elope!"

Why did all the guests frantically leave the cemented swimming area when the man who made his living shooting billiards ran outside with his cue and jumped into the water?

He was a pool shark.

What kind of
religious practitioner
would make the best
shoe repairman?

A faith heeler.

What do you call
a single woman
whose words, on the
surface, appear to be
true, but upon closer
examination prove
to be false?

Miss Nomer.

What did the man say when he looked out his window and saw thousands of ducks and geese winging their way across a blustery, rain-filled sky?

"Looks like
Fowl weather."

What do you call a person who records the location of little wagons on a map?

A cart-ographer.

From what medical condition did the clock repairman suffer when he worked on too many different kinds of clocks?

Diverse-tick-ulitis.

From what psychological condition did the man suffer when he entered a room jam-packed with people wearing Santa costumes?

Claus-trophobia.

From what foot infirmity do astronauts suffer at Christmastime?

Missile toe.

What do you call
informal speeches
given by Christmas
gift decorations?

Bow Talks.

What did one ancient stringed instrument say in response to another ancient stringed instrument's utterance of a falsehood?

"You're a lyre!"

What did the
accordian say
in response to a
question he could
not answer?

"I'm baffled!"

What do you call
a porcupine who
always lags behind?

A slow poke.

What do you call a domesticated feline who has one more than eight stories to tell?

A cat-o'-nine-tales.

What do you call a machine for hurling domesticated felines through the sky?

A cat-a-pult.

What do you call
an elixir made
from ground-up
domesticated felines
that puts you into a
death-like sleep?

Cat-a-tonic.

What do you call
a support column
carved with images
of domesticated
felines?

A cat-a-pillar.

What do
domesticated felines
use to style their fur?

Cat-a-combs.

What do you call
your father's sister
who sells LSD?

Aunt Acid.

What do you call your father's sister who installs sewer systems in the county?

Auntie Septic.

What do you call
your mother's sister
who runs an ice
company?

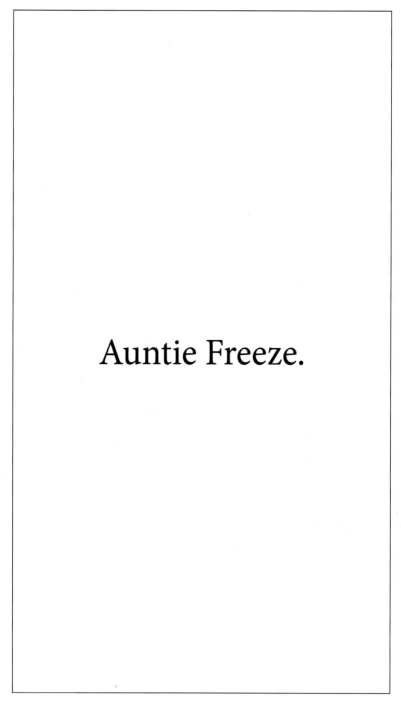

Auntie Freeze.

Why were the ten groups of 100,000 male deer laughing and dancing?

They felt like
a million bucks.

What do you call
a safe designed to
protect long dowels?

Pole vault.

What do you call two identical structures standing side-by-side which extend over a body of water and to which ships are often secured?

A pair-a-docks.

What do you
call two identical
falsehoods uttered
in unison?

Pair-a-lies.

What do you call
two ten-cent coins
sitting side-by-side?

A pair-a-dime.

What do you call identical twins firing rifles at the same time?

Pair-a-shooters.

What do you call diarrhea after a morning meal of coffee and pastry?

An incontinental
breakfast.

What do you call ferocious people with whom you share an apartment?

Vicious roomers.

What do you call a self-propelled, two-wheeled mode of transportation that cruelly and brutally attacks and maims people again and again and again?

A vicious cycle.

What do you call it when identical twins get on identical horses at the same time?

Pair-a-mount.

There is a vehicle filled with people who all ride to work together. What physical ailment afflicts them as they drive through a hole dug through a mountain?

Car pool tunnel
syndrome.

What is it called when the woman who is supposed to deliver your wife's baby at home gets into a serious traffic accident 10 miles from your house, half an hour after your wife's water breaks?

A midwife crisis.

What do you call
a 39.37 inch tall
female domestic
servant?

A meter maid.

What do you call
the past winner of
a prize given by the
inventor of dynamite
to the person who
does the best
rope tricks?

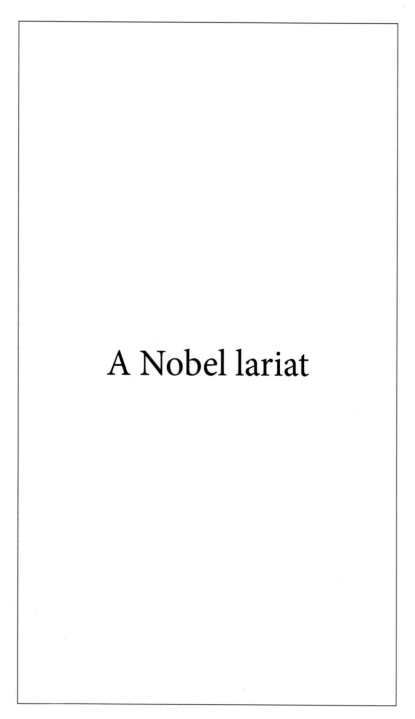

A Nobel lariat

What do you call
the cessation of an
armed conflict when
it is orchestrated by
a barber?

Hair peace.

What do you call it when you force someone to lie down on a folding bed that can be easily carried or stored?

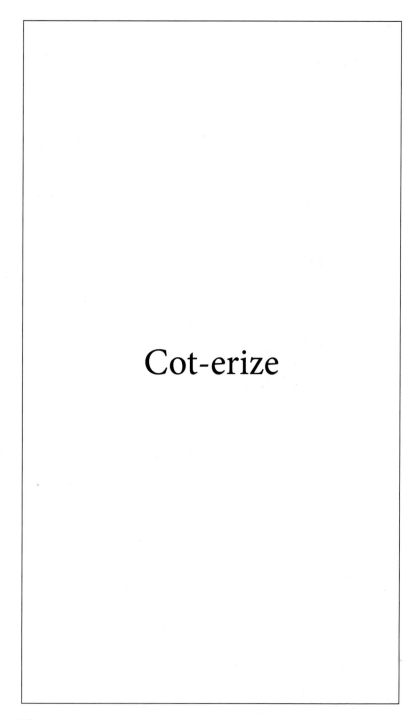

Cot-erize

Why did San
Andreas get blamed
for everything?

It was just his fault.

Why did the election official give Dracula a calculator when it came time to tabulate votes?

He wanted the
Count to be accurate.

Where do large, black, obnoxious birds go to hoist a few after a hard day at work?

The Crow Bar.

What do you call
male sheep when
they are handcuffed?

Ramshackled.

What do you call the islands of sticks, twigs, and plants in which duck hunters hide in Venice?

Venetian blinds.

What do you call the consequences of a male sheep's actions?

Ramifications.

What do you call a male sheep who is smothering pieces of fish with a mixture of flour and eggs in preparation for frying them in oil?

A battering ram.

What do you call
a sharpened baby
sheep thrown at
a whale?

A lamb-poon.

What do you call a device for holding up a solitary mounted, armor-clad medieval soldier?

A one knight stand.

Once a year the man stumbled and fell at work. What did he call the experience?

His annual
business trip.

What do you
call karate blows
delivered by a
baby sheep?

Lamb chops.

What do you call a ship that transports what Dracula drinks?

A blood vessel.

Why did the Man remove the four-legged eating surfaces from his lathe?

The tables
were turned.

What do you call a street where every house is inhabited by a person with a hatchet and an ax?

A chopping block.

What do you call
the calm that ensues
when the planet is
covered with small
green legumes?

Peas on Earth.

What do you
call a length of
interconnected links
that gives orders?

Chain of command.

What do you call a cob with only one large kernel on it?

Uni-corn.

What do you call
the amazing act
of surreptitiously
following another
person without
your shoes on?

Stalking feat.

What is it called when you are mindlessly sketching while eating the most popular candy bar in the world?

Snicker doodling.

What do you call a tropical tree where people go to find a partner with whom to spend a romantic evening?

A date palm.

What was the man trying to do by stabbing the officials who determine cause of death?

He was cutting coroners.

What do you call an education institution that teaches people how to very, very firmly and forcefully pound on doors?

The School of
Hard Knocks.

What do you call a bull's girlfriend?

His significant udder.

What do you call a disaster that occurs at the beach while digging for shellfish?

A clam-ity.

THE
END